Honey

Laura Bruce Watt

Presentation by *BookLeaf Publishing*

Web: www.bookleafpub.com

E-mail: info@bookleafpub.com

ISBN: 978-93-5761-239-5

First edition 2022

This collection is for my family and friends who held me as I cried. You will always be the sweetest part of my life.

This collection is for the hopeless romantics and the heartbroken who cannot see through their pain right now.

This collection is for you. As much as I wish we could have stayed sweet, I will try to never be bitter.

This collection is for the sweetness that I will feel once more.

Lastly, this is for the happily ever after that is still to come.

ACKNOWLEDGEMENT

Thank you to Marieann Joy for starting our literature club over lockdown. It has been the best motivation for me creatively and it helped me fall in love with writing again.

PREFACE

This collection of poetry guides the reader through the stages of a relationship, beginning with the Honeymoon – that sweet but all-consuming time period where you fall so deeply in love that it consumes you.

Succeeding the Honeymoon is the Honeysuckle, named for the beautiful flowers which are also known for smothering surrounding plants. This poisonous flora symbolises how this stage of a relationship is often where the friction starts to emerge. Disagreements can fester, spreading like their own brand of poison.

When a relationship ends, the lingering pain is sharp – like the sting from a Honeybee. Honeybee confronts the aftermath of a breakup, and the pain, confusion, and rejection that follows.

Lastly, Honeysweet explores the eventual realisation that this pain cannot last forever – and that the sweetness you once felt will be yours again.

Honeymoon

Falling in love
Happens
So quickly
That
I can barely
Catch
My breath
As you take
It away.

No Man Is An Island

No man
Is an island.
Yet there
You are,
Floating
In a city
Held
Upon the ocean.
Back home
I can
See the sea
And the
Sea sees me.
Ocean blue
Transparent
To the depths
Of me and you.
In the shallows
We dwelled
For years,
Paddling
Close to shore.
Unaware of what
Lay beyond
Deeper horizons.
Diving into
The depths,

I am unafraid
Of the deeper
Blue.
Staring into
Each other's eyes,
Neither of us
Peering
Into pools of blue
But
Something darker.
Like the view from
The window
The night
We first dove in.
We came
Crashing
In
Like waves.
No man
Is an island.
Yet there
You are,
Pulled out
By the tide
As I stand
Upon the shore,
Waiting for the waves
To sweep over
Once more.

Cusp

For years
We danced
Around
The cloud
Of air between
Our lips.
Countless goodbyes
Rolling off
Our tongues.
On the cusp
I would linger
For a moment,
Considering
What lay
Beyond
The empty space
From my
Mouth to yours.
You were the
Good guy,
There for me
As I cried
Pools of
Tears over
All the
Guys who did
Me wrong.

Saltwater
Clouded
My vision of
All the nights
I spent with you.
But you saw me.
You saw
Every rough
Cut edge,
Like shattered glass
Warning you
To stay away.
Like a broken
Bottle
I was
Swept into
The ocean
As I worked
Hard on healing.
The waves
Rolled over
Me,
Smoothing
Out the edges
Until I was
Soft
Like sea glass,
Ready
To be held

By you.
Now we
Lay together
On the cusp
Of forever,
No space left
Lingering
Between
Our lips.

Soul Mate

Before you
My soul
Was nothing
More than
A bottomless
Pool
Of freezing cold
Water,
Where stones
Could be skimmed
On the surface.
No one was
Ever allowed
To sink in,
No anchor
Had set in
The abyss
Until
I met
The boy
With the anchor
Tattoo.
The one with
Fearless eyes
And a smirk full
Of wonder.
The winning

Combination
That stole my heart
Back then
And now
All the same.
Saying nothing
At all with
The curve of
His lip
Yet saying
Everything
We could never
Verbalise with
His hazel eyes.
With every goodbye
On night drives,
The silence
Grew louder
But years
Of silence can
Be restored
By the thunderous
Reality of
A soul catching
Hold of a soul.
Now as I weave
The curl
Of a lock
Around my finger,

I make sure
To trace
Every edge
To remind
Myself
That this is true.
I am not dreaming.
This is deeper
Than
Boy meets girl
Because this is the
Boy
Who lived
Just across
The road,
Just out of reach.
The boy who
Was too afraid
To utter
"Can you feel it too?"
There was
Something in the air
That said,
Maybe one day.
Now
My soul
Can be ignited
By a single
Glance from

The boy
Who played
Video games
In my childhood
Bedroom,
The one with
Stars
Hung on the ceiling.
Maybe teenage
Heartthrobs
Can be
The soul mate
You always
Dreamt of.

One Year

It all starts
With a spark
As we spin round
With sparklers in
Hand.
I draw a love heart
In the night,
Catching the glimmer
In your eyes.
From awkward
First hugs
In empty car parks
After movie nights
Arranged in
Unsure text messages.
Years of friendship
Building up
To where we are
Now.
Edging closer
As we sit on the
Sofa,
Seconds away
From
Never being
The same
Again.

From first kisses
To seafront
Dates
In old bookshops.
Yet ours will always
Be my favourite
Story.
I dyed my hair
Pink
Just for the
Weekend
As we style in
Matching leather jackets.
The anchor chain
Around my neck
Matching
With the one
Embedded in your skin.
You go
Off to work
At sea
And send
Spotify love songs
To serenade
The lonely days.
Planning our lives
In blocks of three
But there is
Nothing we cannot

Fix with a cup of
Tea
Or red bull tins
To fuel our
Late night drives.
Car seat conversations
Always making time
For Friday night pies,
Just like when
We were younger.
Just friends
Once upon a time
But
Now I am
So glad to call
You mine.

Lifetime

Honey-sweet,
You stir
It into your tea.
You are
Already
Sweet enough
For me.
Honey drips
From your
Lips and
The taste of you
Lingers
On my tongue.
We waste the
Days away
Snuggled up
In cosy blankets.
Movie screen
Afternoons
But no story
Is ever
As good
As the one
We get to live.
Caught up
In your smile,
Your dimples

My favourite
Feature.
I could
Stare at you
All day.
I have
Known
You for
What seems
To be a lifetime,
Yet here we
Are now,
Planning
Our lifetime
Together.

Honeysuckle

Choking,
I beg
For air.
You are suffocating
Me.

I Am No God

If I could
I would part
The seas
So that
I could reach
You right now.
But I am
No God.
Another three
Weeks
Of waiting
Around for
You to come
Home,
Of trying
To be okay
With being alone.
I count my
Life in
One
Two
Threes.
He is home,
He is away,
He is home.
If home is
Where the heart

Is then
Mine is lost
At sea.

Pain

I have known
Love
Like I have felt
Pain.
Burning
Deep in the
Centre
Of my soul.
I feel broken
But I do not
Know if
I have ever
Been whole.
Do you complete me?
I am completely
Unsure
Of everything.
I pick petals
From
Yellow roses
Asking myself,
Does he
Love me?
If this is
True love
Then why
Do I wash

My face
With tears?
I wipe them
Away
And try to be
Braver
Next time.
Rejection
Stings as you
Pour alcohol
Into my open
Wounds,
Mixing a cocktail
Of confusion
That clarifies
Nothing.

Trust Falling

You have me
Trust falling
Six feet under,
Patching
Myself
Together
With the promise
Of another year.

Baby Teeth

You make
Me feel
Like I am
Losing
Teeth.
"Baby,"
Spitting
Bloody
Into
White sinks.
My mouth
Is outgrowing
You.
Honey drips
From your
Lips
As the sticky
Bile
Boils in my
Mouth.
Drowning
In sugar water
As my teeth
Begin
To fall
Out
One by one,

Rotting
From the sweetness
You pour onto
Me.
I can only
Take
So much
Until the
Bitterness
Creeps
In.

Ocean Shore

I keep
Going down
To the
Ocean shore,
With the
Hope
That the
Waves
Will whisper
Your secrets
To me.
I know
This is where
You come
To think.
I wonder
If you tell
The sea
More
Than you
Tell me.
I sink within
The crevices
Of my brain.
I am
Overwhelmed
By the

Thought
That I may not
Consume you
As much as
You consume
Me.
The sea air
Lies
And tells me
That it will
All be fine.
That I will not
Drown again.

Honeybee

A sharp
Pain
Punctures
As you sting
Me with
Your words.

The Rest

I would have
Given
You
The rest
Of my
Life.

Dementia

A few days
After
The breakup,
My demented
Grandmother
Asks where
My boyfriend is.
I tell her
I do not have one.
The confusion
On her face
Lingers
Just like
The feeling
In my bones
As I try
To show
A brave face.
She is forgetful
But
She cannot
Erase
The fact that
We were real.

Weakness

I fractured
My ribs
To tear
My heart
Out
For you.
Cracked open,
I am already
Broken
For you.
I am a mess
Of emotion
And it will
Always
Be my fault.
You are not
To blame
For my weakness.
You are
My weakness.

Muse

I was never
Your muse.
There is no
Melody
To call my own,
No lyrics
Calling out
My name.
Yet there
Is a piece
Of you
In every poem
I write.

Sleep

I cannot
Sleep
A single night
Without
The sound
Of ocean waves
Rippling
Through my room.
I think of drowning,
I think of your
Sheets
And my body
Curled up
Alone.
I fall asleep
Holding my own
Hand
In a shallow
Attempt
To hold
Myself
Together.
You are out
At sea
But you are
No longer
My lighthouse

In the storm.
Saltwater pours
From my eyes
As I flood
The pillow
Trying
To pretend
That this
Is all
Just a bad
Dream.

Push

Everyone
Keeps saying
To push
Into the pain,
But I am pushing
Into a stab
Wound
And I am
Bleeding
Out.

Honey-Sweet

But I will
Rebuild
And it will
All be
Sweet again.

Yesterday

Yesterday was beautiful.
Surprise flowers
Followed by
Poetry under
Fairy lights.
I walked out
Into the rain
And tried
To pretend
That you
Did not break
My heart.

True Love

True love
Is found
In the tears
Of my best friends
As they held
Me and
Cried over
The way
You broke
Me down.

Date Myself

I begin to
Date myself.
My opening
Question is,
What is your favourite
Colour?
As I buy
The red dress
To match
The stain on
My lips.
Soy sauce
Removes
My lipstick
The way you
Used to,
As I sit
At sushi
Conveyor belts
Trying to forget
Your order.

You

I will
Write
For you
Until
You find me.
I imagine
I am sitting
In a café,
Reading about
A couple
In love
When you walk
In.
I imagine
You bumping into
Me in a crowded
Street and you
Stop as time freezes
All around us.
I imagine when
I see you
It will
All make sense.
All the pain
That lingers
In my heart
Will heal

And I will
See
Forever
In your eyes.
I will
Feel the fire
Again
And not be
Burnt.
Within me
Is a modern-day
Romantic
Awaiting her
Once upon a time
With you.

Epilogue
Honey

Falling in love
Happens
So quickly
I can barely
Catch
My breath
As you take
It away.
Choking,
I beg
For air.
You are suffocating
Me.
A sharp
Pain
Punctures
As you sting
Me with
Your words.
But I will
Rebuild
And it will
All be
Sweet again.